Divine Capabilities

KELLY M. DAVIS

WESTBOW
PRESS®
A DIVISION OF THOMAS NELSON
& ZONDERVAN

WestBow Press books may be ordered through booksellers or by contacting:

WestBow Press
A Division of Thomas Nelson & Zondervan
1663 Liberty Drive
Bloomington, IN 47403
www.westbowpress.com
1 (866) 928-1240

Interior Image Credit: Damon C. Davis

Unless otherwise cited, scripture taken from the King James Version of the Bible.

Scripture quotations taken from the Amplified® Bible (AMP), Copyright © 2015 by The Lockman Foundation Used by permission. www.Lockman.org

ISBN: 978-1-9736-7278-4 (sc)
ISBN: 978-1-9736-7280-7 (hc)
ISBN: 978-1-9736-7279-1 (e)

Library of Congress Control Number: 2019912423

Print information available on the last page.

WestBow Press rev. date: 8/22/2019

CONTENTS

INTRODUCTION

Our "humaness" is defined by our Creator's "divineness"
My Humanity vs. His Divinity

Most people today fit in one of these categories: *shakers, makers, takers* and *fakers.*

Shakers are those who have a desire to be heard, accepted and sought after by others. Shakers are typically more outgoing, passionate and vocal. They enter an atmosphere and create movement, friction, and sometimes, tension. To the shakers, this is all right so their desire can be acknowledged.

Makers lean strongly upon their own self-will and strengths. They resolve to force their desire into what they feel is the best way. A maker will convince everyone that a triangle fits into a circle and that it is the best fit. *Takers* are those who have little or no regard for others. Takers are usually driven and fueled by rejection, fear, anger, and covetousness. Last, but not least, *fakers* can be either introvert or extrovert. They are avoiders of true reality, so they live a counterfeit reality. They copy and imitate the things that they desire, and convince themselves that they deserve it. A faker's philosophy is that they aren't hurting anyone or anything because being in control of the thing they desire is what's best.

I was once enslaved to unrealistic realities that had me existing and not living. When I came into the knowledge of the truth of who Jesus is, many of those mental and emotional chains began to break off my life. Accepting Jesus Christ was the starting point of my road to freedom and deliverance.

It took years for me to come into an understanding of my own humanity and embrace this life-changing conclusion. It is impossible to know who you truly are until you know whom Jesus is. Many believers in Jesus Christ don't allow the Son of Man to take part of their daily growth and maturation. I'm talking about up close and personal exchanges, encounters, and daily communion with Him. Jesus said, *"And I will pray the Father, and he shall give you another Comforter, that he may abide with you forever; Even the Spirit of Truth"* (John 14:16-17a). There's tons of treasures, vaults of creativity, talent, dreams and ideas locked up inside of us that's waiting to be unlocked and unleashed upon this generation, and to impact generations to come! The key to unlocking is coming into relationship and alignment with heaven and its custom design for your life. Beloved, the Holy Spirit was sent to be our teacher and guide for this incredible journey! Don't be afraid to truly let go and let God take over!

The kingdom of God is at hand... (Mark 1:15).

Apostle K. Davis

CHAPTER 1
Understanding The Capableness of God

There's a beginning place of understanding God's divine abilities that can only be achieved by becoming acquainted with our Creator. Spending time praying, talking, listening, studying His Word, and communing with Him, these are all vital components to this process. Remember it is a *process.* It is literally a lifetime journey. The word *capableness* means the maximum capable ability, and capacity of a thing. God is ageless, timeless and limitless. There is no beginning or end, so getting to know and understand Him and His ways will never stop. Knowing that He is a spirit, who must be worshipped in spirit and in truth, will help you realize that we cannot use natural knowledge or wisdom to figure out spiritual protocols. First Corinthians 1:1-14 does a wonderful job at explaining that a spiritual mindset is required to access spiritual things. Otherwise, spiritual things will seem like foolishness to a naturally minded (or carnal-minded) person.

Truth can only be found in the originator of divine truth—Christ Jesus. He put on flesh (natural body), came in the flesh (natural birth) and subjected Himself to death (natural suffering) so we would have His capableness coursing through our veins! What love and glory divine! We agree to a divine exchange when we accept Jesus as Savior, God, and Lord. As we yield and surrender our will and ways to His, He takes over as head and leader in our lives. It is through this process that we are stripped—we take off our fleshly, human ways and bring them under subjection to His more superior, spiritual ways. It starts with a decision to put our trust in our Creator, and become who He created us to be. His master plan, a unique one-of-a-kind design is far more superior to any other plan constructed for you or me. We were on His mind and in His heart even before time began. Before there was a physical copy of you in the earth, there was an archetype (original model) of you in heaven. You and I were planned, and predetermined in the majestic bowels of our King of Glory. He created and fashioned us with great intentionality and expectation. We are part of a royal plan and we have royal DNA and blood running through us! If we fail to realize that our weaknesses are His strengths, then we fail to capitalize on His grace, mercy and truth.

For he knoweth our frame; he remembereth that we are dust. As for man, his days are as grass (Psalm 103:14-15a).

My grace is sufficient for thee; for my strength is made perfect in weakness (2 Corinthians 12:9).

We benefit greatly by totally depending on His wisdom, knowledge, views and His power, and learning to live out of that posture. The world looks at this posture as a low, weak and despised posture; however, it is actually an exalted, high posture that places us right where we belong and need to be. Humility and brokenness are key traits that gives access to the spirit of the Almighty to come into our hearts and minds and transforms us into His image and after His likeness. He's the potter, and we're His clay. We must allow Him to have His way. God is a specialist who specializes in fixing broken things. He doesn't discard and throw away broken and shattered pieces, no sir, no ma'am. He takes great pleasure in picking them up, and putting them back together into a wonderful masterpiece. He's an architect, an artist and a magnificent landscaper!

Matthew 23:12 and Luke 14:11 teach us that when we humble ourselves, our God will lift us up and exalt us Himself. Our Father does not take pleasure in humbling us; He asks us to humble ourselves so He does not have to. Matthew 23:12 reads, *And whosoever shall exalt himself shall be abased; and he that shall humble himself shall be exalted.* Jesus demonstrated supreme humility when He was in the earth as Son of God and Son of man. Humility is a necessary trait that we must have in order to please Him. To be humble means to depress, bring low, and to reduce to plain. Our Father does not want us to be emotionally depressed; however, He wants us to step into our sonship. Our human nature is automatically prideful, arrogant, rebellious, and carnal—the complete opposite of what we need to be. Beloved, that outer layer of confidence, self-will, self-perseverance, and selfishness must be banished for Him to work the work He desires upon the tapestry of our lives.

We learn from Moses that his princely, prideful veneer had to be stripped before the Father could use Him to accomplish great things in Egypt, Israel, and in the generations to come. Humbleness of mind is an attribute that takes time to achieve. One must go through a process to reroute their way of thinking. Most times, our eyes will not be opened until we go through certain situations and experience certain lows (Hebrews 11:26).

Esteeming the reproach of Christ is greater than the treasures in Egypt: for he had respect unto the recompense of the reward. To esteem means to respect; admire; value; regard; appreciate; to treasure or favor. Imagine being raised as a prince in the most powerful land where everything was laid at your feet. Your wishes were others commands, and wealth, prestige and honor was your bed partner. Suddenly, you go from living a lavish lifestyle to rags, poverty, rejection, loneliness and depression to ultimately esteeming the reproaches of Christ, identifying with the sufferings of Jesus' life on earth.

How do you suppose he reached such a highly unlikely natural estimation? I'm certain the humbling process that he chose had much to do with that. The Apostle Paul knew how to be both abased and abound. He said, *Everywhere and in all things I am instructed to be full and to be hungry, both to abound and suffer need* (Philippians 4:12). Like most vessels the Father uses to showcase His Glory must go through a humbling process, and acquiesce to the molding and shaping by the hand of our Creator.

Being content in the Lord is simply trusting and knowing that He has your best interests in mind, knowing that He will take good care of you. We must not fight the grueling process; we must allow Him to have control and teach us patience. This helps temper us and makes us more pliable and workable in His mighty gentle hands. Going through His processes helps us come to a place of understanding His capableness and knowing that He is the great I AM who makes no mistakes.

CHAPTER 2

His Capableness

To be capable means having and possessing the ability, fitness or quality necessary to do or achieve a specific thing; to be competent, effective, proficient, accomplished, adept, skilled, useful, talented, gifted, or even accomplished. Capableness goes right to the heart of our ability. Many people can be exposed to similar things, but each one will learn, grasp, and retain different aspects of that same thing.

There are aspects and characteristics about our Creator that we should learn about—things that are beyond what natural learning can impart. One of the Hebrew revelatory names of God is El Shaddai, which means God Almighty. El translates as God or Lord, and Shaddai translates as God, My God, Almighty, even Most Powerful (Ezekiel 10:5; Job 5:17). A creator is greater than what he or she creates because the very thing that's created comes from and out of them. Certainly, things can be created that reach far beyond and influence on a wider and broader scale than the one who started it. *Create* means to begin a thing, to start something brand new, so inherently the thing created has some of its creator inside of it.

The very first verse of the Bible reads, *In the beginning God created the heaven and the earth* (Genesis 1:1). The word *bara* is Hebrew for created, which means to cut down; to select; to do; to shape; to fashion. It also means to give birth to something new of miracles. Keep in mind that our beginning as humans is not our Creator's beginning! Our Creator is the Ancient of Days who is *without father, without mother, without descent, having neither beginning of days, nor end of life;* (Hebrews 7:3).

God was never created, formed or thought up. He is simply that one which is, which was and which is to come (Revelation 1:8). Everything we ever know comes from Him. He is life, and all life comes from Him. Wisdom, time, creativity, imagination, love, beauty and wonder all comes from Him.

El Shaddai/El Shadday

El Shaddai is one of the names of God that emphasizes His all-consuming capacity to be all we need and more than enough. He is the all-sufficient one. He is more than enough. In Scripture, our Creator is also referred to as our maker. Enough means as much as, and as many as what is required or needed; plenty;

sufficient; adequate; ample. The sooner we understand that our God is all of what we could ever possibly need, then we can arise, walk in, and become what and who He created us to be!

The Lord, Our Maker

Our Creator is also referred to as our *maker*. To make means to form something by putting parts together or combining substances. It also implies to construct, to assemble, manufacture, produce, fabricate, fashion, model and to build. Psalm 95:6 says, *O come, let us worship and bow down, let us kneel before the Lord our maker.* There is a special reverence that's due to the maker/ creator from their creation. Naturally speaking, if someone makes something for us, and depending on how special, costly or time-consuming it is, we typically bestow some form of appreciation toward him or her, at least. Usually, our hearts are touched in some manner. The same initial principle applies when we are interacting with God.

Our Creator made us, not because He had to, but simply because He desired to. I wholeheartedly believe there was an expression inside of Him that was so deep and profound that had to be shared. I believe His passion and thoughts towards humankind was beyond anything He had ever created. He made a choice to bring us into life, and to share and display His love for us. There is a difference between what it means to *create* and what it means to *make*. As stated earlier, to create is the first starting of a thing; however, to *make* something is taking and using things that already exist, putting or assembling them together to bring something into existence. We, mankind, were definitely created, but made as well. There had never been a man, human or person made. Our Creator wanted to bring into existence something that had not previously existed.

Mankind was a brand-new creation in the world and was a thought first. Genesis 1:26 states, *And God said, Let us make man in our image, after our likeness:* That was the thought first. He spoke it, released and echoed it amongst the Godhead. The very next verse says, *So God created man in his own image, in the image of God created he him; male and female created he them* (Genesis 1:27). Our wonderful Creator decided to make us like Him that He actually took the very things that makes Him God, to fashion and assemble us largely from what already existed—Himself! This prototype and sophisticated creation was majorly distinct and different from anything that He had already created or made.

Psalm 8:4-5 says, *What is man, that thou art mindful of him? And the son of man, that thou visitest him? For thou hast made him a little lower than the angels, and hast crowned him with glory and honour.* What an incredibly amazing thought!

CHAPTER 3

The Stripping & Ridding of Self

To strip means to remove all coverings from; to leave bare of accessories of fittings; to empty ; to deprive someone or something of rank, power, or property; remove clothes; to undress to disrobe; to pull or tear off; peel off; to scrape off; to dismantle ; to disassemble.

Stripping by definition does not sound like fun, or anything enjoyable to oneself, however it is extremely necessary in process of discovering and coming into alignment with our God's nature and identity. (11 Cor. 5:17) says " Therefore if any man be in Christ, he is a new creature; old things are passed away; behold all things are become new." The moment we accept Jesus into our heart, we receive a new spirit, a REGENERATED spirit. To regenerate means to change radically and for the better, or to generate or produce anew. So,that teaches and tells us that when we accept Jesus we receive a BRAND NEW SPIRIT, and along with that brand new spirit we receive BRAND NEW identity, pupose, and destiny. Old things, meaning former things, past things are from that point on behind us and are no longer to be our reference point and guide. We receive the ability to access new ideas, desires, plans, perspectives, visions, skills, and even strengths. From this place of decision The Holy Spirit now begins to gently and lovingly "show us ourselves" and the " works of our flesh/carnal nature". Coming into this sweet relationship and fellowship with The Lord His love for and towards us becomes our foundation of every decison we make, so KNOWING he loves us unconditionallly enables us to look at ourselves and recognize our need to get "rid" of our own flesh nature and bring it subject to our God-nature(that he installed in us). Without this fundamental acceptance there can be no peaceful exchange of power, because the unregenerated, flesh (natural) nature already doesn't want to relinqush it's reign of control in our lives, it's been the REIGNING KING ON THE THRONE OF OUR HEARTS IN LIVES SINCE WE WERE BORN! When the all emcompassing, supernatural love of The Father manifest in your heart and life the once undispute king (your flesh nature) is K0'd by the new king (Holy Spirit, God-nature). Though KO'd in this initial battle the flesh is a poor looser and does not accept it's DEFEAT, then vows to reestablish itself as reigning champion in the ring of your lives again. So from that moment on their is a consistent and continual fight, brawl, and outright match for the seat of your heart. (Eph. 4:24) says that ye put on the new man, which after God is create in righteousness and true holiness. Verse 25. goes on to say "wherefore putting away lying" this lets us know that in "putting on the new man" which is continuous we must accept God's truth, and rid ourselves of lies, or the act of lying to OURSELVES. Our Creator God is absolute truth, He is The Spirit of Truth(St. Jn. 14:17 &St. Jn. 15:26) in Him is no darkness, lies, or shadow of turning (1Jn. 1:5; Js. 1:17) it's impossible for Him to lie (Heb. 6:18) . With all these things being known and understood about our Creator God he himself actually has provided aid and assistance to us to "help" us with this stripping process. The same Holy Spirit(who in essence is God) comes along and teaches, leads and guides us by showing, and strengthing us in our inner mans so that we can become all that's been planned out for us before the foundations of the world, and that with His help ALL THINGS ARE POSSIBLE! So much encouragement is given unto us as we surrender to Him, that inspite of how difficult, daring, and challenging it may get we keep going and going because we've been give a glimpse of who we are (In Chirst) and where we are going. Good old Faith begins to sprout, spring and grow within our spirits. As time goes on we gain a stronger desire to let go of anything and everything thats against Our Creator God(or anti-God) . The anti-God spirit and agenda doesn't just only seek to go against God, this diabolical spirit seeks to REPLACE God in our very heart,lives, will,passions, and pursuits altogether. If it is successful in replacing Him, by coming against Him with enough key individuals in our communities, schools, systems, businesses, governments, cultures, and nations then it can effectively cause us to become a backslidden generation who no longer carries the blessing and favor of our Creator, some scary thoughts huh. One of stripping definitions is to REMOVE SOMEONE OR SOMETHING OF RANK, POWER, or PROPERTY I must emphatically confess and admit that my most daunting and ongoing fight is with my very own self(me, myself,and I) keeping my self,and my body under subjection to my spirit(living, following, and obeying The Spirit and Word of God) is the most grueling at times, and the difficult daily confrontations. This fight is every single day, and in every decision that you make in your flesh life, you literally choose to "strip" yourself DEPRIVE YOURSELF(FLESH) OF RANK, and control. The Apostle Paul hit it right on when he said " I die daily" (! Cor. 15:21). It's a daily, day by day, situation by situation, occasion by occasion, moment by moment choice and decison to disallow your self to have the preeminence or allow your unregenerated spirit to win. I often think about the so called "privilege" of free will and just like most passion filled believers I've had many moments where I simply felt like" father why did you even allow us to have the ability to choose, and have our own will and ability to disobey you? ' Many years ago I use to wish it wasn't even a possibility,however as I grew in my relationship, fellowship, and understanding of who my wonderful Creator God really was and is, I soon realized His love is so complete, perfect, and undefiled that anything less than Him ALLOWING us to have free will (we could choose life or death, light or darkness, good or evil, ultimately heaven or hell) would be an indictment against who He is, therefore it wouldn't be consistent with His personhood. There's no fear that "they might not choose me", or " they may reject me" or " they may fall away from me" at work in Our Creator at all, whatsoever. He is love an His love is perfect, His perfect love casteth out all fear. (! Jn. 4:18) . Giving us a free will further solidifies His Headship and Godship over all creation, an guarantees that those who receive a place with Him in eternity in heaven have so "met the requirements" by their own selecting,and their own ability to choose their eternal abode be it heaven or in hell.

To RID means to make someone of something free of troublesome or unwanted persons, or things; to be freed or relieved from; to purge; empty; or clear. Ridding also deals with CASTING OFF and AWAY unwanted ways, ideas, and beliefs. I'm reminded of the story of Blind Bartimaeus (Mk. 10:46-52) tells a story of how at a defining moment, Blind Bartimaeus made a choice to "rid" himself of old labels, lies, and a false identity that had held him limited, restricted and isolated. Vs. 46 starts by saying " And they came to Jericho: an as he went out of Jericho with his disciples and a great number of people, blind Bartimaeus, the son of Timaeus, sat by the highway side begging. And when he heard that it was Jesus of Nazareth, he began to cry out, and say, Jesus, thou son of David, have mercy on me. And many charged him that he should hold his peace: but he cried the more a great deal, "Thou son of David, have mercy on me." And Jesus stood still, and commanded him to be called . And they called the blind man, saying unto him, Be of good comfort, rise; he calleth thee. And he, CASTING AWAY his garment, rose,and came to Jesus. What a powerful, defining, and decisive moment that was before Bartimaeus. In that second he had a choice to continue to believe the lie that he had to remain in that blind state and condition OR he could choose to activate his faith, and step out on it(his faith) into the plan, purpose, destiny, and identity that Jesus had waiting for him. He chose well, I believe his God-nature had something to do with it because the bible says that he CAST OFF his garment, which in those days blind people wore a particular garment that identified, and told everyone they were blind. He had wore such a garment for many, many years and lived by all the rules of his blind condition. I believe in his heart Bartimaeus felt like this "might" be his last shot at some sort of "normal" life, and he had heard about Jesus, His miracles, and His power, I believe faith to be healed had swelled up on the inside of him. When his defining moment came he chose God-nature(spirit nature) over the flesh nature. Day by day, week by week, year by year the only destiny, and future his flesh had furnished him was blindness, poverty, and loneliness(he was MARGINALIZED, and PENALIZED for "accepting" this false identity, therefore, sitting on the highway side begging became his way of life.) Very important that you catch that the decision was made before he rose because the sequence of his actions was he cast off his garment(unwanted, troublesome) identity, THEN he rose! Oh, hallelujah, WHAT GLORY DIVINE! Just as it is in our journey and discovery of coming into our own God identity, when we take the first step toward God, He empowers and strengthens us through our faith in Him and we get stronger and more confident in Him and His nature at work within us. The bible records that Bartimaeus immediately received his sight. He was no longer bound,held back, and restricted by the lie that held him captive most of his life, instead he chose freedom, he chose to access his divine capabilities!

SPIRITUAL UPGRADES

To UPGRADE means to raise something to a higher standard, and quality, particularliy for improvement; to reform; to update; to make better; to rehabilitate; to recondition; overhaul; to bring up to code

As stated earlier in this chapter we receive a regenerated spirit when we receive Jesus Christ as saviour, that acceptance trigger's a process, and that process itself is an UPGRADE. The flesh natural (unregenerated nature is our low nature, our base nature, like the basement/bottom). Allowing Jesus into our hearts automatically brings us up, and repositions us, although many times we don't access the full benefits of this upgrade. (Eph. 2:15) says " Having abolished in his flesh the enmity, even the law of commandments contained in ordinances; for to make in himself of twain one NEW MAN, so making peace." Jesus was THE Son of God, but also THE son of man, he conquered and overcame sin IN THE FLESH, and by presenting, and sacrificing His flesh to death by crucifixion he ABOLISHED [to formally put to an end; stop;terminate;obliterate;annihilate] the laws judgments against us. Yes IN HIS FLESH he dealt with the verdict, the sentence, and the penalty waged against us, it was nailed to the cross with Him . Jesus as our mediator made peace and brought reconciliation between Our Creator (Father God) and man(His creation). Enmity is mutual hatred, and hostility against someone or something you oppose. This state of "feelings" existed out of our flesh/human nature towards our divine nature. Being 100% God, and 100% man he was qualified to address, identify, and deal with this issue. Not only did he qualify but he qualified us, and literally REPOSITIONED our "seating" in fallen-humanity, (Eph.2:6) says "And he hath RAISED us up together, and made us SIT together in heavenly placess in Christ Jesus. " that's part of our UPGRADE !!! Jesus's unconditional love that He demonstrated by even subjecting Himself to "put on flesh" BROUGHT US UP TO CODE, and ushered us into a brand new and living way, GLORY TO GOD! By causing us to be positioned, by being repositioned we(humanity) was REPOSITIONED TO ACCESS THE DIVINE NATURE AGAIN. (Heb. 10:20) declares" By a new and living way, which he hath consecrate for us, through the veil, that is to say, his flesh;" Death, destruction, desolation, and denial would no longer rule over us and determine our destiny. A higher standard of living began to place a demand for higher thinking, higher desires, higher planning, and definately higher expectations on our lives. A phrase that I have adopted ASCENDED MENTALITY deals with a mentality that is higher therefore SUPERIOR to our regular,and unregenerated mentality. YOUR mentality is your mind-set, your way of thinking, your outlook, makeup,and disposition in life. Your mentality essentially is what decides where you go, how far you go, and who goes with you in and on lifes journey's with All of it's up's and downs. How we "think" and, what we "think" determines and characterizes our ideas, principles, and our perspectives about life and it's issues, and causes. Your CAPACITY which is the maximum amount that something can contain; your volume; your size; or magnitude, therefore learning to maximize what we have access to is a lesson that I think every person has to go through, because so often we partially utilize our gifts, skills, talents, and ABLILITIES due to a low grade of "thinking" or a low mentality. We settle for things, positions, and places in our life, and it's pursuits that are literally beneath us. Having a low out-look on or about life creates an atmosphere of smallmindedness, limitations, and restricted expectations, so sometimes without even realizing it time passes by and we find ourselves stuck in relationships, jobs,careers, financial dilema's, and many other situations and scenario's that never allow us to TAP INTO OUR DIVINE POTENTIAL, and excel. Living with a base mentality is the breeding ground for stagnation, unproductive, unfulfilled and dull living, which is where we live day by day from a place of "just getting" by and existing but not living life ON PURPOSE or PURPOSEFUL. Jesus said " I came to give you life, and that more abundantly" (St. Jn.10:10). Living disconnected and distant from Our Creator allows our lives to cluttered and filled with futile "things', empty things that take up alot of time, energy, emotions, and in cases money, but do not result in joy, contentment, and real true soul satisfaction. Getting caught up in trying to "fill' voids that only our God-given, God-ordained purposes can fill and satisfy. Alot of times during periods like this we develop ambitions that are not God-centered, and we begin to pursue and "run after" carnal, fleshly, and many times worldy "things" . When this happens it's almost inevitable that you start trying to" keep up with Jones's" or in todays modern times it's "keeping up with the Kardashians". King Solomon who during his life time was the wealthiest and wisest King (1 Kg.10:23; 11 Chr. 9:22), attempted to fill and satisfy his inner longings and yearning by not witholding anything from himself that he" thought" would bring him pleasure, fun, contentment, and satisfaction. Due to his enormous wealth, resources, fame and name there was "nothing under the sun " that he didn't try, in an attempt to satisfy his appetites. (Eccl. 2:10) says "And whatsoever mine eyes desired I kept not from them, I withheld not my heart from any joy; for my heart rejoice in all my labour; and this was my portion of all my labour. In other words King Solomon tried it ALL and had it ALL (sex, women, money, riches, arts, fame,status, position, friends, connections) and in his conclusion he summed all life pleasures and accomplishments WITHOUT real meaning and purpose as VANITY and VEXATION of spirit.(Eccl. 1:2) " Vanity of vanities, saith the preacher, vanity of vanities; all is vanity." Then later toward ending of chapter in verse 14 he says " I have seen all the works that are done under the sun; and, behold, all is vanity and vexation of spirit." Vanity in this hebrew text means vapor, or breath, so in other words its speaking about the "shallow", "non purposeful","empty" " quick" and "futile" existence of something without purpose. At our raw human nature there lies vanity, selfishness, and pride, so it's not hard to find yourself operating from that place of out to please and pleasure oneself, it takes "work" actually to go against it. In some cases vanity will try to masquerade as your defender and advocate. While all the while it's actually "stealing" and "choking" true life out of you! To VEX means to grieve; to afflict; to suffer; or to be sorrowful. So "vexation " of spirit means"spiritual grieving". Think about the hurt, pain, and heaviness of heart you feel when someone you love dies. There's mourning that takes place and sometimes the mourning can go so deep and go on for so long that it's more like you suffering through a death yourself. I don't think a person alive "wants" to feel or experience this, yet in all likelyhood most of us do.Certainly when I matured in life and in my walk with Christ

I understood more clearer King Solomons many attempts to "fill and satisfy" himself were actually attempts to "find intimacy" with his Creator and The God of his Father, King David. King Solomon's relationship, and dealings with The Almighty in it's beginnings were primarily based on his Fathers knowledge, and covenant "exchanges " with God. I believe King Soloman didn't allow his heart to connect fully, and consistently with The Lord,with His Words and His ways. One of the reasons my opinion was formed to this thought was because in all of the glory, fame, favor, and honor that The Almighty bestowed upon Solomon, he one, still wasn't satisfied, two it was easier and easier for him to disobey God's commandments, and direct instructions that he had even spoken to Solomon personally. (1Kg. 11:1-6) " But king Solomon loved many strange women,together with the daughter of Pharoah, women of the Moabites, Ammonites, Edomites, Zidonians, and Hittites; Of the nations concerning which the Lord said unto the children of Israel, Ye shall not go in to them, neither shall they come in unto you: for surely they will turn away your heart after their gods: Solomon clave unto these in love. And he had seven hundred wives, princesses, and three hundred concubines: and his wives turned away his heart. For it came to pass, when Soloman was old, that his wives turned away his heart after othe gods; and his heart was not perfect with the LORD his God, as was the heart of David his father. For Solomon went after Ashtoreth the goddess of the Zidonians, and after Milcom the abomination of the Ammononites. And Solomon did evil in the sight of the Lord, and went not fully after the LORD, as did David his father. Solomon over a span of many many years and most his life was in hot pursuit of what I like to call the "God -spot". One of the understandings that I came to in the Lord some years ago is every person born into the earth, by way of a woman's womb(I have to specify that in this day and age because science, medicine, and technology today seeks to replace God, and His divine order with cloning, and genetic mechanics and engineering) possesses a place that is void and open, and theirs a natural desire to "worship" and "connect" with and to a higher source. Some will admit and say God, or "a god", while still some others will acknowledge by saying " a higher power or source", and theres many that can't explain and just as many that don't recognize or realize so they place themselves, and their own affections and desires in the place where ONLY OUR CREATOR IS SUPPOSE TO BE SEATED! Broadly speaking The "God-Spot" is the place within a person's being that without explanation, knowledge, exchange,or even commitment that that person develops a desire for the unseen, the invisible, the supernatural, and even the "spiritual" world and things.(Jn. 1:9) says" That was the true light, which LIGHTETH every man that cometh into the world." This verse of scripture further strengthens my belief that EVERY single person living, or lived had ability to "divinely connect" with the Almighty. He "lighteth" [to enlighten; illuminate; make see, render evident;

to instruct; to give understanding; to imbue with saving knowledge] How powerful is that, ALL humans have been permeated and saturated within with the KNOWLEDGE OF OUR CREATOR, no doubt about it. It's special built in circuitry, and part of our hard wiring. We have DIVINE ENCODING within our core structure! This unique design and desire can also be what " drives" people to go to psychics, mediums, fortune-tellers, in essence to look to the dark, and occult realm to 'give answers" and seemingly "fill" certain voids, and gaps. The whole reason why the Lord ordained and instituted prophets, and prophetic ministry was so people could have a medium, or channel to communicate and hear from him. The Prophets were and are Father God's MOUTHPIECES, and prophetic ministry is heaven's communication system to earth. When covenant relationships were broken, and The Lord "needed" to speak or talk to His people (The nation of Israel, His chosen people) he would speak to and through one of His Prophets who in turn relayed and gave the message to the people. Israel was delivered, protected, built up, favored, blessed, brought out of bondage, feared, made famous, and EXALTED through and by Prophets and Prophetic ministry. DIRECT communication with Our Creator had to be REESTABLISHED between us(humans/humanity) and Him when Adam disobeyed the original commandment in the Garden of Eden,thereby sentencing the entire human race to a judgment, and curse that demoted us, because not only did he get "banished from the Garden of Eden" (which hosted the presence of God) but he and Eve lost spiritual sight, and the automatic link and connection to the divine. SPIRITUAL BLINDNESS WAS PART OF THEIR, HENCE HUMANITYS JUDGMENT! Relationships, good or bad,or healthy or unhealthy MUST have some form of communication in order to continue. Once that disconnect happened a replacement system was NEEDED for the Creator to speak to His Creation, and the creation to speak and commune back with Our Creator. Prophets and Prophetic ministry was "part" of that extended answer, as well as part of His unfailing love, mercy, and grace. Instead of us (humanity) being struck down, and doomed to curses we were also UPGRADED in this area by Jesus's far reaching sacrifice.

CHAPTER 4

Divine vs. Demonic

In this chapter, we will explore the original plans and purposes of our heavenly Creator. The word *divine* makes many of us think of God, heaven and/or perfection. However, *divine* means like God, angelic, celestial, supernatural, holy, excellent, delightful and supernatural.

In the genesis of time, God created man. He blew His breath into Adam and man became a living soul. Genesis 2:7 says, *And the Lord God formed man of the dust of the ground, and breathed into his nostrils the breath of life; and man became a living soul.* The breath of life refers to the very essence of God. *Breath* means, vital breath, intellect, divine inspiration and spirit. When He breathed into Adam's nostrils, He was literally breathing His divine inspiration and intellect into Adam, thereby placing Himself in the first human being. God divinely imparted divinity into humanity. Wow, what a thought, what a concept, what glory divine! In my opinion, that is partly how *he lighteth every man that cometh into the world* (John 1:9).

This was an inside job, securing accessibility to man's heart, mind, soul and spirit throughout time. This ensured that, no matter what, any and every person on the planet could get in touch with their maker.

Divinity is a dimension that exists within every person. Many people don't know, understand, or tap into this part of themselves. Our natural birth, our life experiences all contribute and help to cover up, and make our divinity obsolete in the earth realm. When something is obsolete, it is no longer used. There's a saying, "If you don't use it, you'll lose it." When you are unaware that something exists, then quite naturally you don't use or take advantage of it, no matter how advantageous it could be to you. The natural birth process is one gigantic playing field for the agents of darkness. Our natural birth is inferior to our born-again birth experience because of the weaknesses of our flesh nature. Our flesh nature is limited and restricted. Satan (the serpent) entered the Garden of Eden to exchange with this fallen nature. This is why our human nature is at a disadvantage against principalities, powers, devils, demons and dark agents. Their makeup is similar in fashion to God, mainly because many are celestial beings who live outside of time, in the invisible realm. They are not tethered or bound with limitations such as our fleshly, weaker bodies.

It was not a mistake, or a secondary thought or decision on our Creator's part to breathe into the nostrils of Adam, giving him a divine ability, accessibility, and capability to be like God.

God desired for us to be like Him, which hints at our god-likeness. This was understood by some children of God, such as Asaph in the Old Testament. Asaph was a musical prophet who penned Psalm 82 as a prophetic song. Asaph was a minstrel in David's tabernacle who had strong intimate relations and beliefs in Yahweh. Nothing else opens you up to receive downloads, upgrades, and revelations from heaven like spirit-filled worship.

In Psalm 82, the very first verse says, *God standeth in the congregation of the mighty: he judgeth among the gods.* In this verse, *God* is the Hebrew word used to describe and identify God [Elohim], the *supreme God.* This can also be applied by way of deference to magistrates, rulers, judges, angels, or even divine ones. Stating that He judgeth among gods [notice small "G"] because we know He is *the* God of Gods, King of Kings and Lord of Lords. The title "God" was used very generically during those times because there were so many gods and idols that many people worshipped and hailed as their god.

The God of Abraham, Isaac and Jacob was specifically called out as such to make the right connection and to be distinguished from all other gods. Before all of that came about, mankind was viewed and acknowledged as gods because of our abilities and likeness to our Creator. Remember, we were created in His image, and after His likeness. No matter how dark and distant our character and ways are, God was still evident within us. I believe His intention was to always shine through us.

He gave us a soul (the mind, will, conscious and emotions)

which means at any time, we could choose ideas and pathways that could lead us further away from being like Him. Yet, He still gave us choices. What love, what confidence in who He is. This is why *he could swear by no greater, he sware by himself* (Hebrews 6:13). There is none greater or could even compare to Him. He knows that we are like gods because He placed Himself in us. In essence, we are gods; little gods, junior gods, chips off the old block.

We're like our Daddy, our Father who art in heaven! Having His nature is a doorway to our own *divinity*. By acknowledging and operating in it, it brings Him pleasure. Revelation 4:11, says, *...for thou hast created all things, and for thy pleasure they are and were created.* The Greek word for *pleasure* in this verse is *thelema,* which means desire, will, choice and inclination. Its We must understand and grasp the idea that our Creator God commands are his desires and will for us.

What He allows to be played out in our lives and in time, can be different. Taking into account that He knows us, and remembers that we are dust, our framework and makeup has limitations. We need a lot of help awakening the eternal realm within us. Even the angels of heaven exclaim in Psalm 8, *Oh Lord Our Lord, how excellent is thy name in all the earth!* That passage goes on to ask, *What is man, that thou art mindful of him? and the son of man that thou visitest him? For thou hast made him a lower than the angels, and hast crowned him with glory and honour.* They stood in complete awe of God Almighty's choice and desires towards *us*, mankind.

There's a level of spiritual understanding that we must ascertain in order to properly distinguish between what's divine and what's demonic. As a born-again believer since 1996, I've mixed up the two many times, especially in my earlier years. Honestly, like most believers, we call certain actions, voices, and decisions God, and actually they are demonic, and things that are God, we refer to them as demonic. It's important to know and understand the roles of soul and spirit, and where *our* desire realm, which controls a lot of our actions, resides and how they work in our daily lives.

The Bible commands us to *walk in the spirit, and ye shall not fulfill the lust of our flesh* (Galatians 5:16). Verse 25 in that same passage says, *If we live in the Spirit, let us also walk in the Spirit.* These are divine instructions on how to maintain victory in our lives. A constant war rages between our spirit and soul. It's not that one is better than the other. It is more like one is automatically connected to our divinity (God), and the other has to be trained and deprogrammed to be reprogrammed from iniquity that we inherited at birth. No matter who you are, we *all have sinned and fallen short of the glory of God* (Romans 3:23).

We are born already attuned to the frequency of sin. We don't have to look for it, turn it on or make a choice—it's automatic. It's all a part of the Adam's fallen nature. In our world today, technology rule today's businesses, markets, and financial exchanges. It is the prevailing and preferred method of handling business. Most of us, without even being tech savvy, understand programming, deprogramming, and reprogramming. A program is a series of planned future events, item or performances. A program also deals with a timetable, a schedule, a calendar, or an agenda. To *deprogram* means to release, undo, eliminate, remove, and also to retrain to deviate from an original series of events set in motion. To *reprogram* means to program anew, to revise or rewrite and usually replace with another set or series.

Our original nativity is from heaven, where we were in the heart of our heavenly Father, who created us. King David said, *For thou hast possessed my reins: thou hast covered me in my mother's womb"* and *"My substance was not hid from thee, when I was made in secret, and curiously wrought in the lowest parts of the earth. Thine eyes did see my substance, yet being unperfect; and in thy book all my members were written...* (Psalm 139:13, 15-16). King David had tapped into a spiritual insight that God had foreknowledge him, and us, before we came into existence!

The Apostle Paul wrote in Ephesians 2:10, *For we are his workmanship, created in Christ Jesus unto good works, which God hath before ordained that we should walk in them.* These concepts were generated from the spiritual realm. Flesh and blood did not reveal these truths to them. However, we must come into a progressive truth that our Almighty God is a spirit, and we must worship Him in spirit and in truth (St. John 4:24). Because our origins are heavenly, there is a program within us.

However, it becomes obsolete, covered and distorted when it's tampered with by sin nature, which elevates our soul to a more prominent, governing part of our nature.

Now we have to talk about the key elements of our soul. Your soul is comprised of the mind, will, emotions, personality and consciousness. It's what makes you *you*! This is quite contrary to those who teach that our souls are no good, low down dirty rascals, and there is no hope for our souls. We may as well shoot our soul and drag it out to the garbage. I totally disagree. Now, I was taught and heard similar teachings and misunderstandings about the soul in my earlier years, also. I do, however, understand that unchecked and undisciplined, the soul is capable of performing some dastardly things. In other words, it is not hard at all for your soul or emotions to lead you into some low places and cause you to make some dangerous decisions. The soul is still just as important as your spirit. Your soul realm is where you live out your faith, and expectancy of God and heaven! Make no mistake about it—without the soul, there's no individual redemptive testimony, and no unique expression of our Creator God.

The Word of God teaches us that the soul and spirit are so close it takes spirit to identify flesh, our soul. In Hebrews 4:12, it says, *For the word of God is quick, and powerful, and sharper than any two-edged sword, piercing even to the dividing asunder of soul and spirit, and of the joints and marrow, and is a discerner of the thoughts and intents of the heart.* This Scripture has given me life. It has helped to clarify many things and situations in my life. Now I know that there are stark similarities and even a cohesiveness that takes place that's pertinent between the two. The Word, which is spirit, is able to differentiate—but not only differentiate, but separate the two very necessary aspects of who we are. They both add and contribute to our overall divine purpose of our lives.

The Amplified Bible, Classic Edition translation of Hebrews 4:12-13 goes even deeper and reveals in more detail the distinction between separating & distinguishing. It says, *For the Word that God speaks is alive and full of power [making it active, operative, energizing, and effective]; its sharper than any two-edged sword, penetrating to the dividing line of the breath of life (soul) and [the immortal] spirit, and of joints and marrow [of the deepest parts of our nature], exposing and sifting and analyzing and judging the very thoughts and purposes of the heart. And not a creature exists that is concealed from His sight, but all things are open and exposed, naked, and defenseless to the eyes of Him with Whom we have to do.* This version really brings it home in describing the application of the Word, which is spirit to the soul realm.

It unveils the truth that there is a dividing line and aspect of the breath of life. The soul and spirit are so closely related that it goes all the way to the depth of our being, that it exposes, sifts, analyzes, and judges down to our very innermost thoughts and our purposes of heart that we may never act upon. Wow!

The Best You...The Divine Version of You

When our Creator formed us and gave us a beginning, He gave us an ability to choose. Our choices are greatly influenced and directed by our feelings, views, understandings, experiences and principles in life. Before we were formed, we were created with an expected end already designed and empowered by God. He saw us finished, completed, accomplished, and perfected before He gave us a body, a name, a title, a family, a destiny, or even an ability to think or make decisions. There is a version of you—the best you, that has already been designed by God and kept in parts of heaven.

God allows us to see previews of coming attractions in our lives. Our lives consist of choices and pathways of thinking that will either lead us into our own will and way, which can bring forth aspects of our true purpose, although not guaranteed. However, following the pathways that are aligned with will of the Father will for sure bring forth our true kingdom purpose and plans. It's like choosing between real and counterfeit.

I don't like fake or phony versions of things. There's very few things that I'm willing to compromise on when it comes to purchasing certain brands or certain foods. Quality becomes a huge factor in making these kinds of choices for things that you desire. Usually, there's a higher, more expensive price tag to purchase the real instead of a lesser quality of a similar product. There are many versions of things. Some people make a living off of imitating famous people by performing at entertainment shows, concerts, TV shows, etc. Even though people can pretend to be you, no one can do the real you, the best you! We only are capable within ourselves of sabotaging this version of us by never discovering and tapping into who, and what we were created to be and do. This happens when we neglect to come into fellowship and union with our Creator. Only He possesses the original script, manuscript and blueprint of our lives. The original blueprint holds and tells our individual stories from our conception to our death. Now this does not mean it's a fairytale. It simply means it is the thought out, planned out desire of our Maker for our lives, with special emphasis on the empowering divine capability of the Holy Spirit working with us.

Every difficult time and place in our lives is not erased. Instead, they are used to build, teach and reveal to us a deeper revelation about our own divinity within us. He never promised us a perfect life or a life without problems. Jesus said, *"In the world ye shall have tribulation: but be of good cheer; I have overcome the world"* (John 16:33). Jesus lets us know that we will suffer, and go through things. Things will not always be how we want them to be. We will have enemies, difficulties and persecutions; however, He stood, defeated and overcame every single obstacle. We have been empowered and divinely infused with the same genetic codes, enhancements and *divine capabilities*!

We must stop accepting and settling for anything less than what's been encoded within us. There's a divine code that's hard wired in us by our Maker. Divine intelligence holds this information and it's accessed via passwords granted to you in your spirit as you study, worship, communicate and walk in fellowship with the Lord. Today's industries are extremely high tech. Everything is password protected to keep sensitive, valuable and even classified information out of the wrong hands. When people don't know or understand the purpose of a thing, there is a high risk of abuse. Jesus said, *"I am the way, the truth, and the life: no man cometh unto the Father, but by me"* (John 14:6). He was stating that the only way to find out, discover and be reconnected back to our original family or identity is through Him. There's no other way!

John 10:1 says, *"...He that entereth not by the door into the sheepfold, but climbeth up some other way, the same is a thief and a robber."* Verse 7 states, *"...I am the door of the sheep."* Hearing and listening to His voice daily through fellowship and communion equips us. It's also during these times of exchange that trusted information, revelation, insight, secrets, password-protected details are shared and unlocked. The more I'm in meaningful fellowship with the Lord, the *more* my desires becomes like His. Each day, I desire to manifest His character and attributes. I desire to bear His image and likeness more and more in the earth. I have a strong distaste for the lesser version of my own will, my way and me. Yet, a burning, stronger desire for *His* version of me. The *best* me is my only pursuit and my new standard whereby all other standards are judged from!

CHAPTER 5

Destiny Bandits: Shattering the Lies of Yesterday

John 10:1 says, "*Verily, verily, I say unto you, He that entereth not by the door into the sheepfold, but climbeth up some other way, the same is a thief and a robber.*" There is always a right way and a wrong way of doing things. There's a right way to handle things, and there is  a right way to enter and exit a place. The right way of entering a place is through an opened door—a "welcome me" door. In the spirit, doors represent access, opportunity, gain, and your destiny and future. They can also be the entrance for favorable or unfavorable events to come and unfold in someone's life. There are legal and illegal doors that must be recognized and acknowledged when dealing with spiritual matters. An illegal door is an opening through someone's mind or emotions after going through some sort of traumatic, or tragic situation such as loss, death, rape, sickness, or any break in their soul.

When a person experiences pain, abuse or suffering, they tend to be delicate, vulnerable and wounded. Therefore, at a time like this, the enemy of our faith, demons, devils, and dark agents are released to come and attack us. They know that the best chance they have is to infiltrate our lies through illegal doors. Illegal doors are entrance and access points that appear during difficult situations as stated before. Most times, we aren't even cognitive or aware of them. They seem to blend right in with our feelings, our personalities, our desires. Certainly at times when we're weak, our judgments and decisions are distorted and off balance.

A *bandit* is an outlaw, a thief, a gunman, and gangster. Bandits break the law and operate outside of its principles, parameters and its power. When Jesus talked about the thief in John 10, He stated that the thief does not come through the door, but climbs up some other way. He plainly stated that the other way is an illegal doorway. Therefore, he's a bandit, a criminal—a trespasser!

Your God-given destiny is very special and has been uniquely encoded with heavenly purpose, intent, vitality and security passwords for protection and access. The Lord has designed us so that we'll possess the ability to access and connect with heaven at any given time. We were created in heaven; therefore our origin is heavenly and not earthly (John 3:31; 1 Corinthians 15:47-48).

Our composition is of heaven, not of earth. Composition is the nature of something's ingredients or its constituents. It is the way in which the whole or mixture is made up—the makeup, the configuration, the anatomy. We were created in the image and likeness of our Creator God. So, by default, we possess heavenly capacity, meaning that built within us is the ability to expand, grow, to house, and host heavenly things.

Because we are made up of heavenly composition, we inherently are able to access, know, understand and synchronize with heaven's plan, purposes, clocks, calendars and timetables. What an amazing and glorious privilege! Ultimately, we are strangers visiting another country. We are spirit beings from heaven partaking in an earthly experience. We must learn and prioritize our heavenly citizenship, and implement the customs and ways of heaven in the earth realm. This is where our true identity spawns from. Our uniqueness can only fully be embraced, accepted and utilized when we begin to center and anchor our lives on this truth! Truth always shatters lies.

"And ye shall know the truth, and the truth shall make you free" (John 8:32). Jesus' statement in John 8:32 continues to ring throughout eternity's past, present and future. Divine truth has so much power that, even if you were born in extreme disadvantage, and unfavorable situations and circumstances plagued your life, such as molestation, rape, poverty, fatherlessness, rejection, incarceration, etc., divine truth finds you or you find it. When you allow it to penetrate your heart and mind, it will provoke an

uprising, awakening, and inspiring jailbreak from the demonic and dark entanglements that once held you hostage. They will no longer be strong enough to hold you in a powerless, defenseless, helpless place. Even yokes, chains and limitations melt at the touch of divine truth!

Jesus didn't just preach, teach, share truth; He *is* the very truth walking amongst us! (John 14:6) This beloved is also why you can't live in a posture of defeat. Once you discover and allow your true identity and native home to define who you are, and how far you can go, heaven will endorse you all the time. You will gain divine clearance to speak and represent heaven on earth. Your voice and authority will increase and rise in the earth, as well as in the heavens. When this revelation becomes reality through application and implementation, you will begin to understand the divine functions of decreeing a thing, watching it become established, and binding and loosing to another level and depth.

As we grow in this grace and understanding, we begin to move and work in harmony and sync with the Holy Spirit. The role of co-laborer takes on a new meaning in our lives. The Bible teaches us through the life of Christ in the earth that Jesus worked with His Father. He did nothing independently or on His own will or accord. Everything He did was heaven centered and purposed! Jesus understood submission, teamwork and cooperation. He lived His life to advance the kingdom of God and its causes, and heaven's plans and agendas.

Certain Scriptures really showcase this strong position. Jesus said, *"My Father worketh hitherto, and I work"* (John 5:17). In verse 19, He said, *"Verily, verily, I say unto you, The Son can do nothing of himself, but what he seeth the Father do: for what things soever he doeth, these also doeth the Son likewise."* The Apostle Paul pushed this same understanding in His apostolic writings to the churches He planted and to some of his fellow ministers in the gospel. *For we are labourers together with God: ye are God's husbandry, ye are God's building* (1 Corinthians 3:9)

When he addressed many of his partners, spiritual sons and daughters, he would call them "true yokefellow, workfellow, fellow laborers, fellow prisoners, and his helpers" in Christ Jesus. Working in unity, with one accord for heavenly pursuits is a consistent theme. It's a method woven through the lives of many and the greatest biblical leaders. It's important that we are conscious and aware that our Father God is ever present and all-knowing. His kingdom is moving forward and advancing right now. There shall be no end to the increase of His government. Although He lives and exist in all tenses—past, present, and future, His gear is always forward and progressive.

Although dealing with our past is something that we all must do, most times, it's not easy. The good, the bad and the ugly issues, circumstances and challenges are all a part of life. However, every single hard and low place can become fuel for future high places, and ultimately weapons of destruction against the enemies' camp and the spirit of the past! The past is two-pronged; it is used to help develop your character, strength, faith, patience and compassion. We must leave it behind and outgrow the place that we once lived in. Yesterday is the past, and should be respectfully placed behind us and not in front of us. It's definitely not allowed to be the dominant voice or influence in our now or future. Our past has the ability to lock us up and hold us back from our God-ordained destiny and future. If we allow the spirit of yesterday and the past to influence our current lives, our now will always be our yesterday. Who we were designed to be from heaven's original plans and purposes will never manifest. In a lot of cases and times, our past was good. We had blessed, favorable experiences, *but* we must never put our stakes down and live there. The truth that Jesus Christ and His gospel brings into our lives is capable of shattering the stronghold of lies the enemy has erected in our lives. It really comes down to us choosing life or death, freedom or bondage, fullness or lack, victory or defeat. The choice is ours!

CHAPTER 6

The God Advantage

Lest Satan should get an advantage of us:
we are not ignorant of his devices
(2 Corinthians 2:11).

Many times, we become very aware of a competing nature that is at work within us. We have an innate desire to win, succeed, accomplish, and to be victorious in all we set out to do. There is healthy, beneficial competition that drives us, as well as mold and shape our character. However, in many cases, if we have not been accepted, loved, affirmed, or have a sense of self-worth, that competing nature will breed insecurity, fears, jealousy, mistrust, stubbornness, and even pride. If any of these characteristics are left unattended, they can sabotage your ability to build healthy, long-lasting, productive relationships.

There are two major influences that are vying for your attention and loyalty. All other influences, voices and agendas all stem from one or the other. I reiterate, there are two major voices and kingdoms vying for your attention—the kingdom of light, and the kingdom of darkness. These kingdoms hold different perspectives, principles and agendas that are perpetuated by various modes of operations that are diametrically opposed and mutually exclusive to one another.

In the kingdom of Satan or kingdom of darkness, the way to succeed is by any means necessary. This includes cheating, lying, shortcutting, pretending and perpetrating while pulling others down so you can go up. This is completely opposite of the kingdom of God, the kingdom of light. In the kingdom of God, the way up is starting down through humility and taking the low road. You start low with hard work, and go through the processes of life. You're always honest, integral and treating others how you would expect to be treated. Many times, Jesus said, *"For whosoever will save his life shall lose it: and whosoever will lose his life for my sake shall find it"* (Matthew 16:25). He drew this parallel often in communicating to His followers just how different the belief systems and ideologies of these two kingdoms differed. When competition is in play, for most of us there's a commitment to emerge victoriously. In other words, the pre-calculated, intended results is to win. To *compete* means to strive, to gain or win by defeating or establishing superiority over others who are trying to do the same. It also means to take part in a contest or to participate.

In the early stages of creation before mankind, there was a spirit of competition that took place in the heavens. Lucifer's, the son of the morning-light bearer, heart was lifted up to where He wanted to take God's place. Isaiah 14 records in detail about the spirit that was at work underhandedly in the courts and hierarchy of the heavenly realms. A breach is a gap or a breaking away of something. This is exactly what transpired in the heavens when Lucifer decided to deliberately challenge his Creator.

Emerging from the kingdom of darkness was the spirit of competition, along with strife, confusion, pride, deceitfulness, lust, rebellion, anarchy and disobedience. Lucifer was so filled and consumed with the idea of being in charge; I believe he experienced two deadly combinations: blindness and forgetfulness. I believe he was so blinded that he forgot he was a created being himself. Therefore, he saw our Creator God in *his* own image and likeness. What a terrible everlasting miscalculation on his part! This major misjudgment doomed him forever, and all whom he influenced along with him.

Jesus stated twice that the servant is not greater than his lord (John 13:16, 15:20a). As believers and disciples of Jesus, we will do greater works in His name. However, doing greater works in His name does not mean we will be greater than Him. Elisha performed greater works than Elijah; however, he wasn't greater than Elijah. It's the same with Joshua and Moses, and so forth. Everything that the successor becomes, does and accomplishes is an extension of the one they served. Now, I know Elijah didn't create Elisha, nor did Moses create Joshua; however, a significant part of the ones who served were created, molded, made, shaped and formed by the hand of the one they served.

These kinds of spiritual principles are based in seeds, producing after their own kind, spiritual fathering, and mentoring, which are very much at play currently in today's church and Kingdom dynamics of relationships. Lucifer made up in his twisted heart and mind to turn many hearts from Elohim (Almighty God) to serving him. His tactics and techniques were filled with strong lust for our attention and affection. Negative, carnal emotions and feelings are perpetuated to cause us to feel inferior, defeated, unworthy, isolated, angry and indifferent. He knows if we stay connected, focused, and locked into a healthy fellowship with our Father, his chances of tricking us into forfeiting our kingdom purpose are slim to none.

The Bible says, *Set your affection on things above, not on things on the earth* (Colossians 3:2). That word *affection* in the Greek is *phroneo*, which means to exercise the mind; entertain or have a sentiment or opinion; to think. Notice that it didn't say affections, but your affection. Every idea stems from one place or influence. So, set, establish, fix, decide every thought in your life toward the furtherance of our Creator's kingdom plans, purposes and pursuits. Furthermore, it's a decision that we willingly and consciously make every day! We choose which kingdom will influence and be perpetuated, reflected and represented in our lives in the earth.

The God Advantage guarantees that if we, *lean not unto our own understanding, but in all of our ways acknowledge Him, that he would direct our paths* (Proverbs 3:5-6). The God Advantage guarantees our heavenly Father's divine hand (His power and rule), His divine guidance (His eyes and heart), and His divine providence (protection, intervention) in our lives. The God Advantage gives us an advantage in every phase of our lives. Whether we are completely aware or not, He is with us and for us when we decide to live for Him and with Him. Advantage is a condition or circumstance that puts one in a favorable or superior position. It means to have the upper hand!

When you have the God Advantage, you have the inside track, which means that you already win. It's a fixed fight. It reminds me of the story in 2 Kings 6:8-12 when the King of Syria was warring against Israel. He was at a complete disadvantage because he wasn't just warring against Israel; he was warring against God's anointed prophet Elisha. Elisha was on assignment from God Almighty. He was the lead spiritual, prophetic spokesman for the Lord during that time. So Elisha was encased in the God advantage; he knew information, details, strategies, what was next, and the plans of Israel's enemies. He was positioned to interrupt the military advancements against Israel. Every time they got ready to advance and gain an advantage against Israel, it backfired. Elisha gave Israel the inside scoop and they were able to avoid certain places and attacks. It happened time and time again until the Syrian king thought he had a traitor in his midst and the heart of the King of Syria was sore troubled (2 Kings 6:11).

Because of his military status, capabilities, skill, size, and knowledge, the King of Syria thought he had Israel by their neck. But what he did not know, and was not attuned to, was the God Advantage that Israel, God's chosen, was covered in. This reminds me of the wiles and snares of the kingdom of darkness and its demonic agents who strategize to stop every born-again believer from advancing in the kingdom of God. Just like the King of Syria, they are at a disadvantage because we are clothed, covered, and moving in the God Advantage! Simply put, we are unstoppable when we are in this mode because we are in sync with heaven's timing, plans and purposes. We already know ahead of every battle, even before it starts that we win. That's the advantage of the God Advantage!

Weapons of The God Advantage

Having the privilege and pleasure to reside in the earth as a born-again believer, as a son of God is my greatest treasure. I wouldn't trade it for anything in or outside of this world. However, this ultimate position also comes with some trials, tribulations and warfare against the enemy and his cohorts of our faith. The word *warfare* in the Greek is *strateia,* which means military service; apostolic career; campaign. Living for Christ Jesus attracts a constant attempt of the adversary to make you give up, give in, and walk away from our Creator's truth and accept his lies. If the enemy can be successful at getting you out of position, immediately disrupting the order and place of Jesus and His Word in your life, that would eventually shake you out of your God-ordained spot and place you into a carnal, man-built spot. A man-built spot is where you now have to depend on the flesh.

Depending on the flesh itself is not only against the order of God, so it is anti-God. It also deactivates the power of God and His Word from lording over our life! Jesus told the Pharisees and the religious community during His ministry period on earth (Mark 7:8), *"...laying aside the commandment of God, ye hold the tradition of men, as the washing of pots and cups: and many other such like things ye do."* Further down, He says in verse 13, *"...making the word of God of none effect through your tradition,"* making it abundantly clear that as powerful as His Word is, it has a divine scope, parameter and protocol that it follows, as well.

Vision

Proverbs 29:18 says, *Where there is no vision, the people perish.* The Amplified Bible translation says, *Where there is no vision [no revelation of God and His Word], the people are unrestrained;.* Revelation is His revealed will toward, for and about us. It reveals His plans and purposes, and causes us to tap into and unlock our destiny and purpose in the earth. Our destiny as a church and nation begins and ends with unfolding revelation. We are taught both from Old and New Testament Scriptures that *man shall not live by bread alone, but by every Word that proceedeth from the mouth of God* (Deuteronomy 8:3, Matthew 4:4).

Revelation, which is akin to vision, must be sought after, received, and then implemented into our lives. The understanding in the Amplified lets us know also that without revelation, the people are unrestrained. Revelation and vision has components that keep us, anchor and direct us. As we are in fellowship and communion with the Lord, the Holy Spirit will show us things and give us insight that we wouldn't and couldn't get apart from His Spirit.

Seeing and knowing what's going on, and what's about to go on, is reassuring in many ways. It allows us to pray and consult with the Father; it can also warn us of pending situations which will allow us to position and posture ourselves for what's next. Vision adds fuel to our lives. It motivates us to look forward in expectation, and to move toward our expected end. It carries hope within it, and urges us towards our tomorrow.

We were born into a family of visionaries. Our royal bloodline is filled with sight, purpose, and intentionality! Our veins are coursing with creativity! Our heavenly Father is the most creative being ever. He has infused mankind with His seer gene. We have the innate ability to see beyond bad, unfavorable situations and to see better and brighter days. We see the good, even in so-called bad people, and in dire circumstances. One of our strengths is this hopeful nature that is encoded within our beings. It is usually inbred within all human beings and remains there until life situations, hardships, negative experiences and fears rip through our lives. In many cases, we begin to hemorrhage, leaking out some of the very fundamental, simple yet important parts of our divine nature.

In Genesis 1, we read how our Father began creating the earth. God saw the devastation and destruction that came upon the earth and He saw beyond it. There was a better day and way. He calls forth a series of things into creation. Verse three says, *He saw the light, that it was good*; in verse 10, He *called the dry land Earth; and the gathering together of the waters seas called the Seas.* He saw that it was good, meaning it pleased Him. In conclusion, God was moving in vision, and in intentionality. The very thing He desired, He saw. And because He saw these things, He was able to *cast vision* upon the earth.

We are also *vision casters*. What we desire, we see; and what we see, we desire. Hope, sight, vision and desire all work together. As born-again believers, our faith is at the helm, working with the Holy Spirit to conduct us on our journeys. Our dreams, aspirations and goals spring forth from this place also. Most of the time, they begin in embryo, seed form; then they grow into various sizes and shapes. Each dream, goal, desire, aspiration, and hope must pass through the prism of vision. Without a vision, the people perish. Without vision, hope dwindles and dries up.

There is inevitable death, yet not always physical death, of creativity, dreams, goals, purpose and destiny. When and if this happens, life becomes "blah." There's no get up and go, no bounce in your walk, nothing to look forward to. You slump into the category of aimless, purposeless day by day living. This scenario can become worse with each passing day until you actually become a bitter, unhappy person. This is the opposite of the life we have been put in the earth to live out. This is partly why vision is an essential part of our divine nature. There's a principle throughout stories in the Bible that I will call, "If you can't see it, you can't have it" principle.

In Genesis13:17, the Almighty God tells the patriarch Abram, *Arise, walk through the land in the length of it and in the breadth of it; for I will give it unto thee.* He promises Abram in the previous verse that He would multiply his seed as the dust of the earth. In the following chapters, God promised to bless his name, his seed, and essentially everything about and connected to Abram. The key to really unlock Abram's faith was that he had to see it. Abram continued to walk with the Lord, and his vision continued to expand. Hence, his revelation of the Lord increased, and got deeper until he actually received a name change. Hallelujah!

His revelation took him through such divine doorways in his faith. Abram believed God for many things and his hope and faith caused him to see and envision. His vision took him from Abram (exalted father) an individual purpose, to Abraham (father of a multitude/nations). Your vision will qualify, shift, and reposition you for greater accomplishments and dreams. It causes you to pursue the very things that you were put in the earth to pursue. Your will and desires marry His will and desire and forges a perfect union!

We see this principle applied in Joshua 6:2. The Lord told Joshua, *"See, I have given into thine hand Jericho, and the king thereof, and the mighty men of valour."* God gave him a particular set of instructions that had to be followed in order to see success. But first, Joshua had to see himself and his army conquering Jericho. I personally believe that if he hadn't seen it, it wouldn't have happened.

Vision and faith are so interconnected, that when the Lord speaks to us, and we receive His words and promises, our spiritual eyes can see what He sees. We are filled with faith to do and accomplish all things that we set out to do. *"Jesus said unto him, If canst believe all things are possible to him that believeth"* (Mark 9:23). Joshua and his army go on to defeat and conquer formidable Jericho with some monstrous odds stacked against them. Vision will be a midwife to your victory time and time again! All glory to God!

Vision is so powerful that it works for favorable or unfavorable outcomes. What that means is that if it partners up with and accepts fear, then in turn it will project fearful images and scenarios before you. You in turn will receive them and believe them. Then your faith is rendered null and void. You begin to succumb to whatever nightmare, torment or calamity you see. We see this in 1 Kings19:1-3 when Jezebel finds out from her husband Ahab that the prophet Elijah has just defeated, made mockery of and killed all her false prophets at the showdown on Mt. Carmel. Jezebel in turn sends a messenger to Elijah to tell him that by a certain time the next day, she was going to either kill him or have him killed.

The problem was that Elijah believed her words. He literally saw it happening to himself, and it birthed overwhelming fear within him. He forgot all about the victory the Lord had just handed to him on Mt. Carmel. Elijah lost sight of the divine capableness of the Almighty, and His sovereignty paled in his sight that moment. During that time period of his prophetic career, Elijah never recaptures his vision, purpose, or the zeal of the Lord for his divine expected end. He goes on to spiral downward into pity and suicidal thoughts. He runs for his life into the wilderness. The Lord then relieves him from his earthly assignment not long afterwards. What we see, is what we believe. What we believe is what we become. Vision, revelation, purpose, sight, hope and faith all work together to bring you to your Mt. Carmel (victory) or your wilderness (expiration).

CHAPTER 7

Divine Reversals

The heavens are set up and con-
ducted like a court system: laws,
lawmakers, court proceedings, ar-
guments, complaints, plaintiffs,
defendants, evidence, and even
verdicts. Of course, there are
presiding judges that govern over
all articles and ordinances, and a
constitution that all parties, and
participants are bound to. Very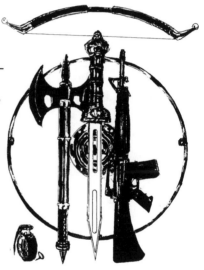
much like natural court proceedings, there's a system whereby
complaints are filed regardless of the veracity or validity of those
accusations. Both plaintiff and defendant are ordered to appear.

And I heard a loud voice saying in heaven, Now is
come salvation, and strength, and the kingdom of
our God, and the power of his Christ: for the accuser

of our brethren is cast down, which accused them before our God day and night. And they overcame him by the blood of the Lamb, and by the word of their testimony; and they loved not their lives unto the death (Revelation 12:10-11).

It clearly tells us where these events took place in the heavens. In the Old Testament, the great patriarchs and many of the believers referred to God in judicial terms. In Genesis18:25, Abraham called him, *the judge of all the earth.* Psalm 96:13 says, *he shall judge the people righteously.* Isaiah 3:13 states, *The Lord standeth up to plead, and standeth to judge the people.* Isaiah33:22 says, *For the Lord is our judge, the Lord is our lawgiver.* Many more Scriptures speak about our Creator and His doings that models a judicial system. Our God is a consuming fire (Hebrews12:29). This means that there is a complete, thorough aspect of His character along with a comprehensive, merciful, compassionate, long suffering aspect of Him as well.

While growing up, I was around a lot of older, seasoned saints and believers. There was a pervading view of how our God was painted to me. It was a painting of a harsh, rigid, unbending, judgmental God. In the last 15 years, I've learned through various experiences that being judgmental and being a judge are two different things. To be judgmental is having or displaying an excessive critical point of view. It means to be fault-finding, condemnatory, disapproving, and overly critical. You may have the natural responsibility via a career as a courthouse judge or some other organization, but never take upon a judgmental character or attitude. That's a trait that not even a natural judge should possess.

A *judge* is a public official appointed to decide cases in a court of law. By contrast, to *judge* means to form a conclusion, or form an opinion. It also means to determine, to conclude and to deduce Judges are supposed to be fair, honest and unbiased to people. Their only bias should be to the law.

As I continue to walk in the ways of The Lord, and growing in His grace daily, I've now ascertained how to give His Word priority to govern my life. The Word of God is a judge that will judge all—believers and non-believers alike. *He that rejecteth me, and receiveth not my words, hath one that judgeth him: the word that I have spoken, the same shall judge him in the last day* (John 12:48). The Father's words, and His will and desires are so pure and full of His truth that once issued, and released from heaven, they carry divine permission—authority, power, and capability to discover and discern! The Lord is not only the judge of all the earth, but He is also a righteous ruler, and a just king. All His judgments are holy and righteous.

John 7:24 says, *Judge not according to the appearance, but judge righteous judgment.* Even here, there was an expectation that we are to judge, but to judge righteously. God and His Word are one; His words carry His very nature and attributes.

The Divine Trajectory of Heaven

In the Old Testament, in there's a dramatic story that gives us more insight about the inner workings of heaven and its court system. In the first chapter of Job, it tells of a transaction that took place in the heavens that directly impacted, and showed up in Job's life. Job 1:6 says, *Now there was a day when the sons of God came to present themselves before the Lord, and Satan came also among them.* It was a time when the sons of God were giving account, in other words reporting on various things and happenings to the eternal judge of all the earth, and when they showed up in this customary manner, Satan himself showed up amongst them to bring charges against Job. Satan was filing a complaint against Job.

The accuser of the brethren was doing what he does best—accusing the children of God. This dialogue reveals Satan's M.O., his method of operation. He literally wanders throughout the earth, looking for a way to instigate and wreak havoc in our lives. Satan launched an allegation against Job that was rooted in materialism and fear. He pretty much accused Job of serving God Almighty because of what the Lord had blessed him with.

The Lord, being light years ahead of any demonic tactic or strategy, gave Satan divine permission to attack Job by killing and taking away everything Job had gained in His life, with the exception of his wife.

Contrary to how many of us was taught about this story, Job had something going on in his heart; some underlying fear was at work in his life that gave Satan legal grounds to gain access to His life but with limitations. Keep in mind that our heavenly Father is the eternal judge of *all* the earth. He is just, and uncompromisingly righteous all the time. There is no darkness or shadow of turning in Him.

Though Satan thought, and thinks still even now that he can turn or change the Father's mind about His children, it is flat out impossible. Our God is the Ancient of Days, and He is omniscient, all wise and all knowing. Therefore, He already knows every development in our lives—past, present and future. Therefore, He allowed this exchange and transaction to go through, and the case was tried. As accusation after accusation was launched, and the case heard, things hidden within Job began to surface and be revealed.

Loss and grief brought him into direct confrontation with the vices of his heart. Through a deep process of humbling himself, Job was vindicated, cleared of all charges, and the judgment was immediate restoration in the form of getting all his goods, belongings, and wealth back. The supreme Judge of all the earth threw in as the best part of His judgment 10 more children, comprised of seven sons and three daughters. The divine trajectory of heaven was already set on a specific course and pathway. Job, being the upright, God-fearing man he was, went through the process—the court proceedings, and was cleared of all charges against him. As a result, a divine reversal was ordered and rendered on His behalf!

«Unique» Superiority

Heaven's function from an operating system is light years superior, advanced, and ranks higher than the earth, to put it mildly. In today's technological world, our cultures, industries, and businesses are inundated with information technology terminology, knowledge, and methods to successfully complete basic life applications, make basic monetary transactions, or socialize or entertain. You have to be somewhat internet and computer savvy.

Heavens Predetermined Plans, His Eternal Passion

Jeremiah 29:11 states, *For I know the thoughts that I think toward you, saith the Lord, thoughts of peace, and not of evil, to give you an expected end.* In this Scripture, *expected* is the Hebrew word *tiqvah*, which is a cord, as an attachment; expectancy; and expectation; outcome. This Scripture is so powerfully encouraging and uplifting. It's one of the most quoted Scriptures in the Bible, yet I still don't think most of the general church population know that the word *expected,* in this text, literally means a *cord.* Let me break it down a little more.

A *cord* is a connector, a link, a tie, something that joins one thing to another. When your heavenly Father formed us, His heart was full of desire to see certain things fulfilled in our lives. Even various key things were encoded and hardwired within our

DNA. We have automatic and default settings. There are many promises and outcomes that will automatically be in your life as a born-again believer. No matter what happens or who comes and goes out of your life, these things will automatically take place. Likewise, with the default setting, after going through different situations, and even growing, and aging naturally & spiritually, we move away from and sometimes get off track or out of alignment with our native kingdom of God citizenship status. We will go through difficult, hard places, and tough seasons that feel like the air got knocked out of us. In some cases, we may have lost our way. It is during these times that having a default setting helps recalibrate and brings us back to a healthy, spiritual setting, and place of identity and balance.

The Father joined and tied Himself to us, which means His heart, and *good* desires are tied to us as well. This means that He himself is inextricably connected to His own wonderful predetermined plans for us! Heaven's thoughts and plans possess the ability, stamina, and the divine capability of manifestation. They are every bit as strong, durable and reliable as He who manufactured and originated them. We are the single most dangerous threat to our divine destiny—*not* the devil, demons, or people. We are. Death and life are in the power of our tongues. So often, we speak demise and destruction out of our very own mouths against our future and destiny. Oftentimes, this happens unknowingly, not fully comprehending the far-reaching repercussions of our words. When this takes place, and it does or will at some point, to have the automatic and the default settings are lifesaving and life changing. Glory to God!

To *predetermine* means to decide in advance, or beforehand. Encoded within the automatic and default settings of heaven's blueprints for our lives are decisions and outcomes that's already decided in the courts of heaven. It behooves us right now to remember our sovereign Creator's eternal position and presiding seat over His creation, thereby not being bound or subject to time, ages, space, matter or emotions. Our Father's intentions, thoughts and hopes for and toward us are good, and not evil, to bring us to a victorious, triumphant outcome. In the end, we win! Having pure, unadulterated passion for a thing can be uncontrollable and the fuel of many pursuits and ambitions.

Passion can work for or against us, depending on our level of discipline and understanding about the trajectory or direction of our lives. Unrestrained passion can lead us too far, too fast. It can take us places we don't yet possess the capacity to handle or maintain. However, working with and harnessing our passions can add extra zeal, commitment, energy, strength and careful concern for those pursuits. A strong craving, yearning, and enthusiasm can be utilized to move ahead successfully into our God-ordained destiny and prove to be extremely beneficial. Passion can be so dynamic and explosive that when left alone, it can turn against us. Acts 1:3 describes the spectrum of Christ's sufferings, all that He experienced and subjected himself to, as His passion. He allowed himself to be scorned, rejected, lied on, spat on, turned against, misunderstood, betrayed, beaten, and separated from His Father and heavenly seat. Ultimately, he was killed because His passion was for His Father's thoughts, plans and desires to come forth. That passion overwhelmed all other desires, and remains top priority in His divine queue.

There is potentate truth and potentate promises that accompany these truths. We know that when God speaks a thing into existence, that very thing spoken or released can't return to Him void. It must perform, and execute His desire. His words are truth, because He is truth. His words are also powerful. *Potentate* means unlimited power; possessing great power and sway; a monarch or ruler; having complete power. In accordance with His character and attributes, our Creator's truths are impregnated with divine promises and divine purpose that carry and house His power and authority. These attributes are like heavenly supplements and appendages in the realm of the spirit. They add extra guarantee and assurance that His kingdom will come and His will be done in our lives.

It's invigorating to know at any point and time in our lives, heaven has access and ability to order divine reversals in our lives. No matter what's railing and raging against us, or tries to sabotage our success or advancements, Heaven can overturn or veto any decision, at any time, and reset our lives to our automatic and default winning settings! All glory to Jesus!

CHAPTER 8

Acknowledge, Awaken and Arise!

As for me, I will behold thy face in righteousness: I shall be satisfied, when I awake, with thy likeness (Psalm 17:15).

Being in deliverance ministry for over 20 years, I have learned early on that you cannot cast out what you do not acknowledge! Casting out demons and devils is the removal and eviction of something or someone that's no longer welcomed or wanted in a particular residence, body, object or location. As a deliverance minister, I was taught that there has to be an open communication, understanding, and acknowledgement that something is present. This divine authority and ability of casting out and removing demonic, wicked entities is part of the divine endowment given to every believer. We find it in Mark 16:17, which says, *And these signs shall follow them that believe; In my name shall they cast out devils;…* It's a list of five divine enablements and to cast out devils is at the top of this list!

Our heavenly Father is not only interested in the saving

of your soul; but He's committed to seeing you set free from demonic entanglements and evil influences so you may shine and thrive in the earth. We are His prized possession. He has invested glorious treasure inside us. This treasure is buried under constant attacks of the enemies of our faith. Heaven's ultimate desire for our emancipation from the molestation of our enemies and the core of deliverance is not so we can just be saved, but so that we can effectively advance and perpetuate His kingdom in the earth. This is very difficult to do being in bondage to the very system and kingdom that opposes His! This is why true deliverance ministry is paramount and a must.

Along with prayer and prophetic ministries, deliverance ministry is one of the most fought ministries in our churches today. Even the kingdom of darkness knows the procedures, protocols and powers of our divine nature. When Jesus walked the earth, He cast out more devils and demons than our King James Version of The Holy Bible records or can hold. He taught His disciples and apostles to do the same. The kingdom of His Father could not come fully into the earth and be established without such confrontation. In Matthew 12:28-29, He teaches, *"But if I cast out devils by the Spirit of God, then the kingdom of God is come unto you. Or else how can one enter into a strong man's house, and spoil his goods, except he first bind the strong man? and then he will spoil his house."* A couple key things that need to be pointed out here:

1. There must be clashing and confrontation of kingdoms.
2. The kingdom of God and light can't fully operate until devils and demons are removed.

When darkness has control or influence over your life, the true light of heaven within you is doused or hidden. You've lost your flavor because you're not being the salt of the earth. You're dull and ineffective instead of being the light of the world. Nothing makes you shine and radiate the glory of our Father and His kingdom like true freedom. Deliverance from darkness is necessary in order to fulfill our kingdom mandate.

Wake up! Wake up, Oh Glory!

There's another manifestation that comes along with being under the control or influence of the kingdom of darkness and that's being asleep. Sleeping and going to sleep naturally is imperative and even essential to healthy lives and cell regeneration. However being asleep in the spirit can have debilitating, grave consequences. While we are asleep, we are unaware, not alert, and unresponsive to many things taking place around us and in our world. Though sleeping is an important part of our Creator's programming design to refresh, renew and refuel us, when we're spiritually sleep, it gives the kingdom of darkness and all their inner workings time and room to slip things into our minds and lives, ultimately with intentions to deceive and destroy our advancements.

In the New Testament, the Apostle Paul would often make references to the condition of being sleep or asleep. The Greek word for *sleep* is *hypnos.* It's where we get the word, *hypnosis. Hypnos* means spiritual torpor, under. It refers to an inferior position. When you are spiritually sleep, you are inferior to every tactic and device of the enemy. Previously, I wrote about how we were created to be superior in every way. We are the head and not the tail, above only and not beneath. Being spiritually asleep deactivates this position. Through process of degrading, you are repositioned and an attack is launched against you to stop and block you from discovering this travesty.

Hypnosis deliberately blacks out your thinking and impairs your comprehension and cognitive abilities. Your mind becomes a blank piece of paper and whomever is controlling the hypnosis can write and ingrain upon the walls of your mind whatever they want. Whether it's for you or against you, good or evil, beneficial or not, they are in charge at that moment. The problems is what's enacted, and activated into your being now has the ability to show up in your life. When we are waking up from a night's rest or even a good nap, we are initially slower in our responses. Sometimes, even our equilibrium takes a few seconds to get balanced. So it is in the spirit world as well.

When we are asleep, we are at a major disadvantage as to the scheming of the powers of darkness. Because our judgments, vision and hearing are also impacted by this condition, we call good evil, and evil good. We accept and allow harmful, toxic things entrance into our lives. We don't see what we need to see resulting in an inability to make healthy choices. Our hearing is polluted and diluted, so we move on partial or wrong information. This goes on and on until we are comatose and totally unresponsive to the hand, touch and divine purpose! In Romans 13:11-13, Apostle Paul warns of this debilitating condition:

And that, knowing the time, that now it is high time to awake out of sleep: for now is our salvation nearer than when we believed. The night is far spent, the day is at hand: let us therefore cast off the works of darkness, and let us put on the armour of light. Let us walk honestly; as in the day; not in rioting and drunkenness, not in chambering and wantonness, not in strife and envying.

He teaches that night acts like a cloak of darkness. At night, generally we sleep. However, He is saying we have been asleep too long. We have been inactive too long. We have been incoherent and unresponsive for too long. As a church, we have been lukewarm, passive, and not aggressive about our outcome for too long! He even tells us in the last verse of this chapter to *put on the Lord Jesus Christ* (Romans 13:14), letting us know it is a decision that we all have the ability to make.

Other places in the Bible talks and warns about being asleep. *Therefore let us not sleep, as do others but let us watch and be sober* (1 Thessalonians 5:6). We understand that *sober* means the opposite of being drunk or intoxicated. Being sober also means to be calm, collected and circumspect so we can think properly. Being sober, vigilant and watchful is a posture that is needful in order to stay woke and not to become prey to the powers of darkness. The Bible likens being asleep to being drunk. Even the Apostle Peter warns us. *Be sober, be vigilant; because your adversary the devil, as a roaring lion, walketh about, seeking whom he may devour* (1 Peter 5:8). Being sober, woke and alert helps prevent the devil from getting a stronghold in your life.

The enemy is very proactive about stopping you from your tapping into your divine nature and capabilities. Therefore, he literally roams, seeks and stalks the corridors of your life looking for an entrance point to see if he may devour you. Even he knows the choice is yours; so part of his plan is to deaden your senses and your understanding of spiritual matters. He wants to get you disinterested, and lethargic concerning your kingdom assignment. He wants to sabotage and short circuit your knowledge of Christ. In order to prevent this, we must be sober and watchful. Jesus told His disciples to watch and pray!

When you watch in the spirit purposely, it is done with amazing results. When you are watching, all your senses are heightened. It stirs and arouses a level of boldness and aggression that is needed for safe and secure objectives to be met. It's impossible to truly watch, and be passive about it. The very nature of watching is a type of strict discipline. To *watch* means to be active, and give attention to. The gates of hell cannot prevail against a church or a person who is attentive and cautious. That's why they want you sleep. To *watch* also means to be sleepless. This means that I am wide awake, cognitive, aware, and ready to participate.

Time to Arise

Beloved, the very last thing the enemies of your faith want you to do is to arise from your sleep. When you come out of a spiritual sleep or stupor, there is a realization of time that you have actually lost and can't get back. In a lot of cases, this is catalytic and gives birth to a passionate stance against what had you enslaved. Usually there is fervor and a strong desire to never fall asleep like that again, and to go after that, which capitalized upon your sleep condition.

To *arise* means to confirm; to be clearer; to accomplish; decree; perform; remain; to stir up; be strengthened; to succeed and to become powerful. You were marked for greatness the moment you came into the earth. That mark was identified by your opponents. It was a struggle for many of us to arrive in the earth, due to medical, emotional, economical, and even relational family challenges. Many plans were set in motion to try to block you from being born! *But God!*

Our brilliant Creator had no intention on you living an unremarkable life. Your life was, and is ordained to cause a stir in the earth realm. You're ordained to part Red Seas, and to break wide open the religious stereotypical, racial and sociological boxes designed to keep you operating minimally. It's time to arise! Arising within yourself is a type of spiritual awakening. Once you awake, you must act upon the unction and revelation that has risen with you. When you awake, the life of God and His Spirit begins to flow and move through you. Your eyes, ears and mind are now opened and cognitive.

Cognitive deals with your ability to know; to perceive and process, which all are important in you moving forward. Once you acknowledge and awaken, the next step is to *arise*. King David, who was a skilled warrior and worshiper, penned these words: *Let God arise, let his enemies be scattered:* (Psalm 68:1). Throughout the psalms, David calls upon God to arise and defend, arise and judge, arise and have mercy, arise and bless. David knew many wonderful things about the Lord of Glory, and one of those things was that winning had to be within him, and his destiny!

It is time to stand up, stand out, and live on purpose and by purpose! You were formed, fashioned and strategically placed in the earth to shine. You're more than a mere spark; you are a flame loaded with potential to become a consuming, blazing fire. You were sent to add flavor, pureness and authenticity to our world today. As you go, grow, embrace and explore why and what you were born and created to do, be willing and ready to discover new things and ideas about yourself and others around you. Your placement in the earth was by unique intent. The community and city you live in is in need of what you possess. The school you attend, the career or job you occupy is waiting on you to come forth and emerge with the zeal, passion, and ability of heaven. Marriages, families and relationships stand to be healed, mended, and restored by your touch.

So what are you waiting for? Make a decision now to divorce the old ways, old habits and old ways of thinking. Old unproductive methods will keep you in bondage and out of your true kingdom purpose. There is a "not so" within you and now is the time to release it and let it out!

CHAPTER 9

Heaven's Arsenals

The heavens are not only filled with information, revelation, divine intelligence, and promises, the heavens are loaded with power, authority and weapons of mass destruction! The heavens contain many different departments, agencies, levels and dimensions. There's also rank and order that facilitates and administer its ordinances, laws, decrees and rulings. The heavenly realm is where everything originates from. It's the source, the genesis and starting point of all we know that exist, that's recorded and verified. Before there was this earth that we live upon now, there was former earth. The first one existed before Genesis1:

In the beginning, God created the heaven and the earth, and the earth was without form, and void; and darkness was upon the face of the deep. And the Spirit of God moved upon the face of the waters. And God said, Let there be light: and there was light (Genesis 1:1-3). Although not taught and understood in most Christian churches, this piece of Scripture actually captures and tells of the act of our Creator creating another earth or, recreating and bringing restoration and order to earth.

In Genesis, there was huge time and space. Many different events took place that is not obvious, and requires deeper study, along with reading other writings, particularly the Jewish Talmud, and other historical documents. These writings explain, and fill in many gaps to our western American limited revelation of the God of the Bible, particularly regarding the inception of time as we know it. Upon studying, praying and listening to solid revelatory teaching over the years, and allowing the Holy Spirit to teach me, I've come to understand that there were civilizations and inhabitants of the earth before the first chapter of Genesis. Other places in the Bible that shine some light on these truths are in the prophetic books of Isaiah, Ezekiel and Revelation (Isaiah 14:12-20; Ezekiel 28:12-19; Revelation 18). There is a deeper, expanded understanding that you have to be diligent in prayer, focus and study to unearth some biblical mysteries.

In my opinion, you need to read more than just the King James Version of The Holy Bible, along with contemplative prayer to accurately grasp, digest and handle these truths. The heavenly realm is superior to the earth realm. It's not subject to time, nor the laws that govern our earth. As an example, time and space are laws and concepts that we respect and adhere to. These laws help govern and keep order in our earth. They also dictate our lives, relationships, societies, cultures, science and our currency exchange of money. Gravity teaches us what goes up, must come down. As a result of this law, things are grounded, and not flying all around. These same laws do not exist in the heavenly realm. The heavenly realm is also called the *spiritual realm*, the *supernatural realm* or the *divine realm*. I have heard it referred to by other names as well; however, in this chapter we will call it the *causatory realm*.

To *cause* means to produce, to generate, to make happen, to induce, or to begin. Everything that happens in and on the earth is a direct result of an activity, movement or decision from this realm. A *realm* is simply a domain, a kingdom, or a sphere that is ruled by something or someone. Heaven is a kingdom, and its rulership and government is under a king, with a theocratic form of government. The eternal king that rules heaven is Jesus. *Of the increase of his government and peace there shall be no end, upon the throne of David, and upon his kingdom, to order it, and to establish it with judgment and with justice from henceforth even for ever* (Isaiah 9:7).

Time, being a nonfactor in the heavens, very often when something transpires in the heavens, it has to be processed through time in the hearts and minds of us in the earth. This is due to limited revelation and understanding of this incorporeal realm. Most of our societies, industries, businesses, and cultures in the earth were built and generated from shallow and/or inaccurate, or incomplete knowledge of this extraordinary supernatural realm.

Cause and Effect

Sir Isaac Newton's original Third Law of Motion describes that for every action or force in nature, there is an equal and opposite reaction. This fact is part of basic physics, mathematics and science. The "cause" or what makes something happen, and the "effect," the result of what happened or transpired is engrained and imprinted in our human relationships, and interactions all throughout our world. If there was no cause and effect, life would be motionless, stagnant, passionless, very unfulfilling and will eventually die out. Cause and effect is not only a law, but a spiritual principle that's enforced. It carries and releases a compound effect while in action. Lots of things inherently within them possess a divine ability to accelerate, grow and gain as they move. As our wonderful heavenly Father's prized creation and possession, everything we do has some sort of reaction and calls for a response. The delicate, unique gift of life originated from the Law of Cause and Effect. Simply put, without an action, a cause can't be revealed, known, acted upon or fulfilled.

Because is an interesting concept and wields great power, implications, and influence throughout humanity. It is the catalytic vice that stirs, creates, and releases feelings, actions and thoughts. It is responsible for most actions and reactions. The word *because* is a conjunction, which means for the reason and since. *Because* is the cradle from which passion, ideas, motivations and inspirations are birthed cultivated and germinated. Our designer the Creator planted within us an automatic response system that is activated by stimulation. Most times, stimulation comes in the form of actions. Stimulus is an event or thing that evokes a specific functional reaction. The stimulus itself is the catalyst and we are responders. A touch, a kiss, a hug, a kind word, a negative word, a smile, a laugh, even a sneeze, cough, or wave could be an action or a response. Our divine capability is so multifaceted, and sophisticated that millions of other actions and responses keep our lives moving along.

Let's look at some basic Biblical examples:

And God said let there be light, and there was light (Genesis 1:3).

And the waters prevailed exceedingly upon the earth; and all the high hills, that were under the whole heaven, were covered (Genesis 7:19).

And Adam knew Eve his wife; and she conceived, and bare Cain, and said, I have gotten a man from the Lord (Genesis 4:1).

And Moses brought forth the people out of the camp to meet with God; and they stood at the nether part of the mount. And mount Sinai was altogether on a smoke, because the Lord descended upon it in fire: and the smoke thereof ascended as the smoke of a furnace, and the whole mount quaked greatly (Exodus 19:17-18).

And it came to pass, when he made mention of the ark of God, that he fell from off the seat backward by the side of the gate, and his neck brake, and he died: for he was an old man, and heavy (1 Samuel 14:18).

Now when Solomon had made an end of praying, the fire came down from heaven, and consumed the burnt-offering and the sacrifices; and the glory of the Lord filled the house (2 Chronicles 7:1).

And Jesus, when he was baptized, went up straightway out of the water: and, lo, the heavens were opened unto him, and he saw the Spirit of God descending like a dove, and lighting upon him: (Matthew 3:16).

For God so loved the world, that he gave his only begotten Son, that whosoever believeth in him should not perish, but have everlasting life (John 3:16).

How God anointed Jesus of Nazareth with the Holy Ghost and with power: who went about doing good, and healing all that were oppressed of the devil; for God was with him (Acts 10:38).

While Peter yet spake these words, the Holy Ghost fell on all them which heard the word (Acts 10:44).

And I saw a new heaven and a new earth: for the first heaven and the first earth were passed away; and there was no more sea (Revelation 21:1).

Again, these are just a few basic examples of cause and effect in our Bible. It would literally fill hundreds, perhaps thousands of books if we were to share every Biblical example of cause and effect. As it is in our life cycles, cultures and societies today, so it was throughout the biblical ages, and quite frankly since the inception of time.

Our wise master builder very intentionally designed us and gave us the gift of life. Life's idiosyncrasies, mysteries and unexplainable logic on purpose knitted us finely together to be impacted and affected by what we do and don't do. It's a fine, delicate balance working between all forms of life. This ensures that we rely on one another. We're eternally and naturally connected to each other's choices, whether profitable or unprofitable. Our human body is composed of trillions of interdependent, interconnected actions and reactions that's absolutely vital to growth, maturation, development and continuance of life.

As the Apostle Paul describes in Ephesians 4:16, *From whom the whole body fitly joined together and compacted by that which every joint supplieth... Fitly* describes the unique way that we benefit from one another in the body of Christ. I love that we are called the body of Christ. Throughout the New Testament, we find this description used to explain particular functions, roles and administrations. So perfectly joined together we are, that our actions and reactions are life giving, sustaining, and can be depleting. To every action there is an equal and opposite reaction! What we do matters; but so does what we do not do. Our codependency is part of heaven's design.

Superior or Inferior

Due to heaven's ideas, passions and intentions, we were fashioned to dominate and have dominion. Dominion courses through our spiritual veins. We inherently possess the code of dominance and triumph. One of my coined phrases that I have shouted and declared for years is, "We know no defeat, only victory." In the beginning, we were commanded to *have dominion over the fish of the sea, and over the fowl of the air, and over the cattle, and over all the earth, and over every creeping thing that creepeth upon the earth* (Genesis1:26). Make no mistake about it, this was a commandment—not a suggestion, not a proposal, or recommendation. We are dominators by birth. We were created intentionally superior over all other creation. Reigning and ruling was imbedded in us.

Let's think for a second. The Father created other amazing, stupendous things at the time of creation besides mankind. He created the heavens, the earth, sun, stars, and moon; fish, fowl and cattle. As His chosen representatives in the earth, He gave us governance and authority to be fruitful, multiply, to rule and subdue. The fact that He also commanded us to subdue is an indicator that there would be opposition and resistance. However, we were the superior species. The word *dominion* is *radah* which means to tread down; to subjugate; to prevail against; to reign; to rule. Dominion is a very powerful act and responsibility. We are head and shoulders far above all creation, known by man and unknown, in this world and world to come.

Being created in His image and after His likeness definitely guarantees that we possess the capacity to win. That's a part of our *divine capabilities. Superior* means higher in rank, status or quality. 1 John 1:1-2 distinguishes His love toward and for us. The Amplified Bible version goes into a deeper description: *See what an incredible quality of love the Father has shown to us, that we would [be permitted to] be named and called and counted the children of God! And so we are! For this reason, the world does not know us, because it did not know Him. Beloved, we are [even here and] now children of God.* I like the usage of the word *quality* in this verse, and not just quality, but incredible quality! Glory, hallelujah!

It even goes further to talk about the remarkable opportunity that we've been given to be permitted and allowed to be named and called His children. This truth by itself separates, distinguishes and places us in a category alone, and higher than all His creation. With this status, those of us who live for and with Him are always victorious. Infused with the authority, power, protocol and majesty of heaven, we are also His weapons here in the earth against the continual onslaught of hell. We are heaven's weapons of mass destruction. We're ambassadors and agents on assignment here in the earth realm.

Part of our divine commissioning is to stand against and take down the works of darkness. The body of Christ operates as armed forces with militaristic attributes, mindsets, skillsets, disposition, and tendencies particularly the apostolic and prophetic branches of this military. Me being an affirmed and confirmed apostle in the Lord's church, by functionality I know, understand, and move in these dynamics daily. We are in a continuous war; therefore, we must know, embrace and engage in warfare in order to impact communities, cities, and nations to advance the kingdom of God in the earth...to occupy til he comes! (refer to Luke 19:13).

The word for *warfare* in the New Testament is *strateia* which is where we get our English word *strategy*. It literally means military service and the apostolic career as one of hardship and danger. 2 Corinthians 10:4-5 tells us, *(For the weapons of our warfare are not carnal, but mighty through God to the pulling down of strong holds;) Casting down imaginations, and every high thing that exalteth itself against the knowledge of God, and bringing into captivity every thought to the obedience of Christ.* Verse 6 goes on to say, *And having in a readiness to revenge all disobedience, when your obedience if fulfilled.* An integral part of our "warfare" is obeying the instructions, and the will of our Commander in Chief, Jesus Christ. by revenging which means to retaliate, vindicate, protect, defend, and to punish against all of the enemies of the Lord and His kingdom. Operating at this level is not mean, hateful, or wicked; it is in fact fulfilling part of our divine commissioning. If we only do part, and not whole, then we are not compliant with the orders of our Commander in Chief. Therefore, we are being disobedient and are noncompliant.

The kingdom of light/God and the kingdom of darkness/Satan are diametrically opposed and mutually exclusive. They are always clashing. Even though Satan is no match, and powerless against the Almighty God, the One who created him, he does have some power, which is now illegal. He is influenced to move, act, and assault people in the earth. The Apostle Peter puts it like this: *Be sober, be vigilant; because your adversary the devil, as a roaring lion, walketh about, seeking whom he may devour* (1 Peter 5:8). Although we have been given *power to tread on serpents and scorpions, and over all the power of the enemy* (Luke 10:19), a part of our treading on is in the posture of standing, and contending.

To *contend* means to strive or vie in a contest or against difficulties; to assert; to maintain; to hold; to claim; to profess; to declare; and to pronounce. When we contend against the kingdom of darkness, we are staking our claim on the words, ordinances and laws of the kingdom of light. Contending is a declaration of our faith in the sovereign God, and His capableness. We are literally pronouncing judgment upon the enemy. All glory to King Jesus!

With heaven's divine arsenal and its weapons of mass destruction at work on our behalf, they are very formidable and basically unstoppable at annihilating their opponents. Partly why Jesus came into the earth realm, and became a man, in flesh, was to engage in this very necessary warfare that could only be legally waged, and won by a son of God, a man. Warfare at this level was inescapable. The charges, indictment, and sentencing against the human race was severe, and the ramifications far reaching, beyond any person's lifetime, family name, generation, status, financial strength, power and human intellect.

No person living possesses the complete package or the capableness to neutralize, atone, or appease for the charges of sin laid against us. Christ Jesus is not only our Commander in Chief, but He was and is the Advocate and Mediator with the Father, Creator God on our behalf. He fully gave Himself to the mission of rescuing the human race. During the time of certain negotiations, He gave His life as ransom for all. Jesus' sacrifice was for *all*, though all won't accept Him, but many will.

A *ransom* is a price, ultimately an exchange to reconcile, fulfill or satisfy demands during a hostage situation. Technically, the human race was being held hostage by the terms and conditions of the disobedience in the Garden of Eden. We were down and out for the count and in need of a Savior. Knowing who and whose you are, are key to accomplishing your pursuits and goals. Not knowing who you are devalues you, and diminishes your self-confidence, thereby opening doors of fear and unbelief, causing you to stop moving forward. One of the strongest, most reliable and consistent supplies of strength flows from the reservoir of knowing why you were born and what you were sent in the earth to do. If and when we arrive at this point, it will alter our perception, sharpen our focus and fuel our days with fresh passion and zest for life.

Purpose is inherent and interwoven in our DNA and courses through our veins. When it's active, it will draw, lead, guide, inspire, convince, block, reroute, and even teach us. Purpose is vital to our overall wholeness. Not being in touch with your purpose has been a factor in people making shipwreck of their lives. Purpose grounds and anchors us even during the storms of life. Purpose will keep you from drowning and sinking.

One of my favorite conversations in the Bible is when Jesus stood before Pontius Pilate. Their dialogue is loaded with so much raw truth, revelation, inspiration and fighting ammunition that to this day and every time I read it releases fresh insight and direction.

> *"Jesus answered, My kingdom is not of this world: if my kingdom were of this world, then would my servants fight, that I should not be delivered to the Jews: but now is my kingdom not from hence. Pilate therefore said unto him, Art thou a King then? Jesus answered, Thou sayest that I am a king. To this end was I born, and for this cause came I into the world, that I should bear witness unto the truth. Everyone that is of the truth heareth my voice"* (John 18:36-37).

Powerful, powerful, powerful! Arguably, during one of the toughest times of His life, Jesus doesn't bow or bend to the dictates of the flesh. He did not lose sight of His purpose, nor did He devalue His mission in the earth. While being persecuted, His divine nature shined brighter and stood head and shoulders above all other plans, agendas, ideas, motives and power sources.

Our King Jesus was married to His purpose; there was no separation or division. As he stood betwixt two purposes, God's and man's, He stood in absolute integrity and wholeness! We need clear hearts and minds in order to walk and live successfully in the earth realm today. There are so many voices, ambitions, and desires all around us, and it's easy to get taken off your God- ordained pathway. You are not a mistake or born by happenstance. The hands of a loving, passionate, creative designer who knows all about you planned your life deliberately and intentionally.

You are a custom design, tailor-made for greatness. You are crafted for uncharted success and accomplishments. You must tap into the divine reservoirs of heaven's streams by talking, praying and dialoguing with our wonderful Creator. Allow Him to disclose and download information and revelation about you and His plans for you. You will be amazed at the capableness that lies dormant within most of us. Get ready to be unlocked and unleashed in our earth today!

God bless each and every one of you for taking the time to purchase and read this divine inspiration. My prayer is that you come to know the greatness within you, and to fully recognize your divine nature. Then and only then, will this world get the opportunity to experience and witness your *divine capabilities*!

Pray this prayer with me,

Father, I come before you in the matchless name of Jesus. Please forgive me for living a mediocre, average, apathetic life distant and separate from my divine nature purpose in the earth. I ask that you would come and fill my life. Utilize me the way you desire to. I ask that the very reason that

You created me and sent me into the earth would emerge to help me to recognize, embrace and connect with my true purpose.

Father, please remove all scales from my eyes. Remove all limitations from my mind and imagination, and remove all unbelief and fear from my soul so that the fullness of your desire toward me can manifest in my life. I want to accomplish and achieve what I was born to accomplish and achieve. I am a world changer. I was born to dominate, reign and rule with a breastplate of righteousness. Father, recalibrate and attune me to the frequency and sound of heavens and to the marching orders assigned to me in the earth today. Deactivate any and all false sounds, harmonies, and rhythms within and around me until they have no effect. Lord, I want to know You more intimately, personally and deeper. I want to know Your ways, reveal them to me I pray. I thank You and praise You. In Jesus' mighty name! Amen!

Printed in the United States
By Bookmasters